RETURN TO CIVILITY

A *SPEED OF LAUGHTER* PROJECT

RETURN TO CIVILITY

A *SPEED OF LAUGHTER* PROJECT

JOHN SWEENEY &
THE BRAVE NEW WORKSHOP

Return to Civility © 2007 John Sweeney

ISBN 978-0-9762184-2-5

Library of Congress Catalog Number: 2007940675

Published in the United States of America
Printed in Canada

First Printing: November 2007

11 10 09 08 07   5 4 3 2 1

Cover design by Ryan Huber Scheife
Interior design by Jeni Henrickson

Aerialist Press, or Publishing Without a Net
Minneapolis, MN
www.aerialistpress.com

Dedication

To all the people we work with at the Brave New Workshop. We are all so blessed to be surrounded by people who remind us through their daily behavior how to live a civil life.

A special thanks to our editor, Jeni Henrickson, who takes our improvisational thoughts and turns them into something wonderfully readable.

Prologue

This summer, my wife Jenni Lilledahl and I were at a concert for her birthday. The artist was Grammy-award-winning folk singer/songwriter Shawn Colvin—she is Jenni's absolute favorite performer! It was a beautiful evening at the outdoor amphitheater at the Minnesota Zoo. The audience consisted of about 1,500 adults, mostly in their late 30s to mid 50s. They were regular folks, nice folks—"Minnesota nice" folks. Shawn took the stage and began to perform, and her first three songs were some of Jenni's favorites. Jenni and I held hands, resting them on my knee, and reflected that after nine years of marriage, we are still in love, with two beautiful, healthy boys, and here we were watching Shawn Colvin and everything was right in the world. Well, almost everything. In the middle of her third song, Shawn abruptly stopped playing. She stopped because, unbelievably, she had to ask this crowd of upper-middle-class, educated people to please reduce the volume of their conversations so she could hear herself in her own stage monitor.

I was steaming—furious at how disrespectful these people were being toward such a wonderful artist, furious at how disrespectful they were being toward the people who were listening to her, and furious at how disrespectful they were being toward my dear Jenni. Unlike my wife, my ability to differentiate between my emotions and actions is somewhat flawed. But just as I was about to take action (whatever foolish thing that would have been), Jenni lightly squeezed my hand and said, "Remember, they're not trying to be rude, they're just forgetting to be civil." As usual, she was compassionate, insightful, and right. I immediately realized I had to do something; I had to get rid of the anger and start being helpful. When there was a break in the concert, I walked outside the amphitheater and left myself a long, detailed voicemail describing my idea for this book you're about to read.

Within a few days, I typed up an e-mail describing what happened at the concert and my idea for this project, and I sent it to the fifteen or so wonderful people Jenni and I work with at the Brave New Workshop. I asked them to please help me come up with 365 things we could all do to make this a more civil world. Using our improvisational culture, our whole team went into a whirlwind of thinking and writing and talking, and we soon came up with these 365 ideas. I love working at the Brave New Workshop!

We wrote this book as a reminder to ourselves to be thoughtfully civil, and as a reminder of how simple that can be on a daily basis. We also wrote this book as a pledge—as an organization, as a team, as a group of improvisers, we pledge to practice as many of the civil behaviors contained in this book as we can.

We hope you enjoy this book and find it helpful. We also hope it energizes you to think of other ways to increase the civility in our world. If you think of a couple of new ideas while you're reading, please go to www.speedoflaughterproject.com and help us write the next volume of *Return to Civility*!

Thank you!

John Sweeney and the Brave New Workshop

1

Be the "yes person" for those around you.

When your friends, family, or coworkers have an idea, need to talk, want feedback, or just need a listener, be the "yes person"—the person who listens with an open mind and always says "yes, I can see your side of it" or "yes, I can help you with that" or "yes, I can see how that might work" or "yes, I am listening."

2

Shut your laptop during meetings.

Give everyone your full attention. They will appreciate it, and you will be better informed.

3

If you RSVP to attend an event, plan to show up.

Or let the organizer know as soon as possible if your plans change. Your RSVP could trigger decisions that cost money and time, including food purchases, logistics, and staffing. Remember too that there may be someone on a waiting list who would be happy to take your place.

4

Park wisely and courteously.

Don't take up two spaces. Don't park in handicap spots unless you're authorized. And if you're vying for a parking spot with another driver, let the other driver have the spot while you seek out another one.

5

Return phone calls and e-mails.

If someone calls you, return the call. If you receive an e-mail, let the sender know you received their message. If you can't answer an inquiry right away, let the sender/caller know you'll get back to them with an answer (and follow up when you can).

6

Wear clothing that respects and honors the situation.

Dress up for religious services, parties, and events. Honor a situation by taking time to look nice.

7

Ask more questions and do less talking about yourself.

Take the opportunity to learn something new, to learn about someone else, and to open your mind. Help make someone else feel good about who they are and what they've accomplished.

8

Pack out what you pack in.

This applies to many situations, not just camping. If you visit someone else's office, take your half-drunk coffee out with you.

9

Smile.

Behind every smile is the potential for a new adventure in friendship and understanding.

10

Let people who've had a positive impact on your life know what they've done for you.

Even if it's been years since you talked to someone and you feel guilty about having been out of touch, bite the bullet and contact them.

11

Share your knowledge and passion.

Teach someone how to play a sport or game or how to build or create something. Spread your joy.

12

Be the organizer.

Instead of waiting for someone else to step forward, volunteer to be the organizer. Choose an area that you feel passionate or confident about. Share your time for the benefit of others.

13

Send as many thank-you notes as complaint letters.

Take the same amount of time to praise great service as you do to complain about bad service. Recognition of work well done is a great self-esteem booster.

14

Don't answer your phone if you're engaged in conversation with someone.

This includes text messages and e-mails. Keep your eyes and ears focused on the person you're with. If you're expecting an important call that you can't miss, ask the person you're with for permission to answer it: "Sorry to interrupt, but may I take this call quickly? It's important." Then get off the phone as soon as you can.

15

Try to think of new or unexpected phrases of gratitude.

Instead of "please," "thank you," "excuse me," and "you're welcome," try "my pleasure," "not at all," "I appreciate it," "much obliged," "I beg your pardon," "how kind," etc. People hear the typical phrases so much, they sometimes lose impact. The really old-fashioned phrases may even make people smile.

16

Get out and volunteer.

Go to a nursing home, hospital, library, food shelf, humane society, or school. Volunteer the things that you can: money, time, books, food. Make the world a better place for someone else.

17

Choose to give your business only to companies that give good service.

If you're not happy with someone's service or a company's policies, don't do business with them. Go one step further and tell them why you're not using their services. Your actions might result in helping them improve.

18

Send a handwritten card or letter.

In this electronic age, a handwritten note holds more weight than ever before. Taking the time to write to someone will make that person feel very special.

19

Listen to more than one source of news.

Try to get a balanced perspective on a topic before forming an opinion about it.

20

Walk down your local street and pick up all the trash you see.

Think of the number of people who won't have to see that trash the next day, including yourself.

21

Let the person with their blinker on into your lane of traffic.

Think how much you appreciate it when someone else does this for you. There's nothing more frustrating than being unable to get to your destination because other drivers are hogging the road.

22

Use your blinker before you make a turn—every time.

If we combine this with the practice of letting people in who have their blinker on, we may have just solved the traffic problem in two steps.

23

Delete junk e-mail and chain letters on the spot.

Don't forward them to family and friends. Everyone gets too many e-mails already—help lighten the load. You can even take it a step further and report unsolicited e-mails to the FCC. Perhaps if we all did this, we'd be able to stop spam altogether.

24

Strive to be on time.

If you're going to be late, call to let those who are waiting know. Time is money. If you let people know that you're going to be late, they can choose to reschedule or work on other things while they're waiting.

25

Give unsolicited hugs to family members.

Remember how your parents used to embarrass you with public displays of affection in front of your friends? It's payback time.

26

Be generous with compliments.

It's wonderful to feel loved and appreciated.

27

Learn and practice the art of waiting patiently.

As the old saying goes, "If you waited nine months to come into this world, you can wait twenty minutes for a hamburger."

28

Every single day, be thankful for at least one thing in your life.

Try to pick a different thing each day. It can be as small as a warm pair of socks or as big as a life without oppression.

29

Thank a cop, firefighter, or airport security officer for helping keep us safe.

Show some respect for those people who put themselves in harm's way for your safety.

30

When traveling, follow carry-on baggage guidelines.

If you take up twice as much space as everyone else, the message you're sending out is: "I'm more important than you."

31

Get to know your neighbors, and remember their names.

If your house catches fire and you're not there, your neighbors will be the ones calling 911.

32

Be mindful of the volume of your cell-phone conversations.

Other people are trying to carry on conversations of their own. And none of them wants to hear what you did last night.

33

When you're in line behind an elderly person at an ATM or airport check-in kiosk, be patient.

They have seen more technological changes than any previous generation. Treat elderly people in the manner you hope to be treated when you are seventy-five and rushed.

34

If you have an issue with someone, talk to them directly, not behind their back.

You'll never be able to resolve the issue unless you bring it out in the open. And if it's not worth resolving, then it's probably not worth discussing—with anyone.

35

Believe in something beyond yourself to keep your ego in check.

Sometimes simply looking at a picture of Earth taken from space is enough to remind you that there are more important things in the universe than your crisis of the day.

36

Thank your teachers.

Send them a note and let them know that many of the things they taught you have been helpful. If there are things they taught you that you didn't understand until recently, let them know that too. Thank them for their patience and let them know their hard work paid off.

37

If you borrow something, return it as soon as possible.

Your friend may not think about it again until she needs it and is tearing apart her house looking for it, so make sure she has it back before panic hits. And be certain it's clean and in working order when you return it.

38

When you're getting on a bus, train, or plane, choose to be the last one aboard.

You'll spend less time in a crowded vehicle, and you'll be one less person exhibiting "me first" behavior.

39

Pray for peace.

Someday we'll learn to resolve conflict without violence.

40

Believe that every action you take affects the world, and take responsibility for your actions.

If you drop a pebble in a pond, a butterfly in India might win the lotto!

41

If you're unsure if you'll be able to make it to a meeting, let the organizer of the meeting know.

Tell them that you're still deciding and will get them an answer ASAP. Set a reminder for yourself to follow up, and make a decision as quickly as you can.

42

Clean up after yourself
in a public restroom.

Wipe up any splashes or drips you make, pick up dropped towels, and don't forget to flush.

43

Try to avoid watching TV or reading the paper for twenty-four hours.

It's hard to keep an optimistic, positive outlook when you're being over-whelmed with negative images, stories, and stats, so take a break for a day and focus on what's great about your family, friends, and coworkers.

44

Learn how to use the blind carbon copy (BCC) feature on your e-mail composer.

It shows you respect people's privacy (you're not broadcasting their e-mail address to others), and it makes your message more personal.

45

Push in your chair when you leave a table.

Why stop with your own chair? Be a good chair steward and make life less of an obstacle course. You might prevent an unforeseen accident in the meantime.

46

Say please and thank you for big and little things.

Repetition becomes habit, and good manners elicit respect.

47

Learn a foreign language.

It's a big small world. If we all learned even one more language, think how much more clear communication we could all have.

48

Be aware of others around you when you're driving.

Make decisions based on safety and courtesy instead of how late you are for a meeting or how eager you are to get home from work.

49

Keep moving when you're exiting a busy plane, elevator, or room.

Don't stop to pull out your cell phone or chat with your friend. Get outside the door and move to an open, out-of-the-way place so that others can continue on to their destination without having to wait for you.

50

Have your money ready at the drive-through or check-out counter.

Thinking ahead to the next step makes any line move faster.

51

Give a coworker a small token of recognition for work well done.

Bring in some flowers, a short note, a cookie. Recognize someone's hard work and accomplishments. Think how nice it would feel if someone did this for you.

52

Make sure the volume of your conversation is appropriate for the location.

In the words of your favorite preschool teacher, "Use your inside voice."

53

Shop local and support your local economy.

The heart of a community is in the support they show for one another.

54

Respect people's personal boundaries without judgment.

Not everyone is comfortable hugging. Maybe they were brought up Lutheran. It doesn't mean they don't like you.

55

Listen when someone is talking, and let them finish their train of thought before you speak.

Really listen. Don't just mentally compose your response. You might learn something.

56

Accept the mistakes of others graciously, knowing you make mistakes too.

You never know when you'll need someone to return the favor.

57

If you notice someone needs help, offer assistance.

The first step is to pay attention to those around you so that you notice when someone needs help.

58

Stay home from work if you're sick and keep your germs from spreading throughout the office.

The amount of work hours lost in a round-robin sickfest is far greater than the loss caused by your absence.

59

Practice hope.

Even if you don't believe in hope, you may eventually trick yourself into being a hopeful person.

60

Use golf etiquette in real life.

If you're in a situation where there are many people in line behind you, hurry as quickly as you can so others don't have to wait too long, but don't rush those in front of you.

61

Ask an elderly relative to tell you a story from their past, even if it's the hundredth time you've heard it.

If you really listen, you may learn something new. Maybe your grandma dated Mussolini.

62

When you go up for seconds at a buffet, ask your tablemates if they want anything.

Don't you appreciate it when someone offers to save you a trip—especially when you're wedged into a tight space between tables or seated on the inside of a booth? Plus, you'll burn calories while you help.

63

When it snows, shovel a neighbor's sidewalk too.

What a marvelously easy way to build a positive relationship with your neighbors.

64

Stay awake in class.

You're much more likely to learn something, and much less likely to irritate your instructor.

65

Take time to recognize and appreciate the small things in life.

Life is not much more than a long string of small events anyway.

66

If you're taking care of a friend's pet, spend time with the pet.

Don't just rush in, put food in the bowl, and rush out. Give the pet some quality attention and time. If you don't think you can do this, then don't agree to take care of the pet.

67

Read.

Books are engaging and inspirational. And they make you smarter too.

68

Practice general hygiene.

Cover your mouth when you cough. Wash your hands after sneezing into them or whenever using the restroom. Brush your teeth and keep your mouth smelling fresh. You get the idea.

69

Say "Excuse me."

Say it when you burp, pass gas, sneeze, cough, bump into someone, need to work your way through a crowded room, etc. Others around you will appreciate the gesture.

70

When you're getting on an elevator, stand back and let everyone off before you get on.

You'll get on the elevator sooner than if you try to fight the flow of the crowd. And you can't start the elevator until everyone's off anyway.

71

Exercise patience and understanding while traveling.

If people are laughing and enjoying themselves while you're trying to finish typing up a sales report, try to exercise patience and understanding instead of snapping at them. If novice travelers in front of you are trying to figure out how to work the electronic kiosk, help them out.

72

Respond to emergency relief calls for donations.

The urgency of the situation should be enough to motivate you to help. If it's not, remind yourself that bad things can happen anywhere, anytime, and to anyone—including to you.

73

Learn to read others' body cues.

Is the person sitting next to you reading? Are they trying to sleep? If so, they probably don't want to talk with you. Sometimes being friendly means being quiet.

74

Put your carry-on in an overhead bin near your seat.

How would you like it if, when you arrived at your seat at the front of the plane, the bin above your row was full of luggage from people in the back? Keep your carry-on near your own seat.

75

Listen respectfully to people with different opinions than yours.

You may be persuaded to change your mind, or you may find that their statements further strengthen your resolve. In either case, you'll gain new perspective.

76

Get off your cell phone while conducting transactions.

The girl selling you a sweater at the Gap doesn't want to wait for you to finish your conversation about what to have for dinner so she can ask for your credit card. Try putting down your cell phone while conducting transactions. If you receive a nonemergency call mid-transaction, let the caller know that you'll call them back when you're finished with your transaction.

77

When declining another person's offer, be direct, honest, and polite.

It's like pulling off a bandage. It may sting for a second, but it'll be quickly forgotten.

78

Be the person who always has what someone else needs.

Keep aspirin, safety pins, a lint roller, and other handy items in your desk drawer, and share them with your colleagues.

79

Give blood at least three times a year.

Go for the sake of others, stay for the orange juice!

80

Wash the dishes or load the dishwasher without being asked.

Face it, dishes need to be washed and it has to be your turn some-time—unless, of course, you don't use dishes, in which case you're off the hook.

81

Thoroughly clean the snow off your car before you get on the highway.

It's never good if you can't see out your own car windows, and when that piled-up snow atop your car flies off at high speeds, it can be a hazard for the drivers behind you. Driving in or after a snowstorm is tricky enough as it is.

82

Recycle.

Consider future generations and how this simple choice can change the world even after you're long gone from it.

83

Take turns and share focus.

Remember that there is plenty of time after a meeting or discussion to share additional thoughts in an e-mail or letter.

84

Hand out blankets and food to the homeless.

There are so many opportunities to help, and so many charitable organizations to support. If everyone helped out just once a year, perhaps there would be fewer homeless people.

85

Keep Bluetooth technology out of public spaces.

If you're standing in line at the bank, having a conversation via your Bluetooth, people around you may think you're talking to them, which can be embarrassing and frustrating. It also closes you off from the rest of the world, and you'll never know what you're missing.

86

If someone's cooked a meal for you, eat some of it even if you don't like it.

Don't put too much on your plate if you're unsure whether you'll like it. And don't make a big to-do when trying something you've never eaten before.

87

Turn over the remote to someone in the house who rarely gets to control it.

Turn it over, let it go, and keep your thoughts to yourself. Decide to be happy with whatever the person chooses.

88

Actually look outside when you hear a car alarm go off.

Don't just assume someone else will look. Maybe it's your car being stolen. Or maybe your car will be next.

89

Help out at your child's school.

Help shelve books in the library, read to a class, or organize a fund-raiser. Perhaps your child's teacher could use some help cutting out or assembling materials. There are many small ways you can help make your child's school a better place.

90

Surprise an old friend.

Call someone you've been thinking about reconnecting with. See how they're doing and let them know you've been thinking about them.

91

Offer a ride to someone who usually relies on public transportation.

You won't spend much more in time or gas money, but you'll greatly improve someone else's day. And you'll likely enjoy some good conversation to boot.

92

Share crowded public spaces instead of hogging them.

If you want to read a newspaper on a crowded subway or airplane, try pulling out one section at a time and reading it folded in quarters. You could offer the sections you're not reading to your neighbors.

93

Turn off the lights when you leave a room.

Conserving energy is good for your bank account and the planet.

94

Be sensitive to other people's health or dietary restrictions.

Some people can't eat lots of sugar. Others aren't into pork. Vegetarians won't appreciate a meat fest. Some people don't drink and are therefore uncomfortable having lots of booze on the table. Learn people's preferences, and then respect them.

95

Assume that others are having a worse day than you are, and act accordingly.

"I cried because I had no shoes until I met a man with no feet" is more than just a saying.

96

Replace the words "Huh?" and "What?" with "Excuse me?" or "Pardon me?"

Old-fashioned courtesies are pleasant to the ears, and they make you seem smart too.

97

Ensure that everyone in a group knows everyone else's name.

Assume that introductions haven't been made, and just do it. You're also helping out those who need a refresher.

98

When you don't give someone a job they've interviewed for, call them to let them know they didn't get the job.

And when it's possible and reasonable to do so, let them know why they didn't get the job, what their strengths are, and how they might better sell themselves to the next potential employer.

99

Find a way to vent your frustrations other than by complaining to loved ones.

Journaling, yoga, working out, meditating, hobbies—there are hundreds of ways to release your negative energies that don't involve stressing out those you care about most.

100

Bring a gift.

The next time you're a guest at someone's house, bring along some flowers, a bottle of wine, or a selection of tea or coffee. It's a nice way to say "Thank you for having me," and your host is sure to appreciate the gesture.

101

If you see someone reaching for something they can't quite reach, offer to get it for them.

Height is a gift. Share it.

102

Use your best manners around children.

This applies to all children, not just your own. Model good behavior. And by all means, watch your language.

103

Celebrate others' accomplishments.

When you celebrate a person's accomplishment, you're really celebrating the person. What may seem small to you could be a lifelong goal to someone else.

104

Take off your sunglasses when talking with people.

Unless you're standing where the sun's directly in your eyes, remove your sunglasses while speaking with people. Let them see into your eyes, thus removing any suspicion or doubt.

105

Let others go in front of you.

If you're at the ATM and you need to make a deposit, let the guy behind you who just needs to get twenty bucks go first. Likewise, if you're at the checkout counter with a whole bunch of items and the woman behind you has only one item, give her your place in line.

106

Leave complete, written instructions for babysitters.

There's nothing worse than having a screaming toddler demand, "*Backyardigans,*" when you don't know how to work the DVD player.

107

If someone cuts you off in traffic, give the peace sign instead of the finger.

Road rage creates unresolvable anger that you won't be able to shake. And at 60 mph, the other driver might think it's the finger anyway. It's a win-win situation.

108

When attending a social event where you'll be interacting with other people, wash your hands.

Help reduce the spread of germs. There have been studies that if 40 percent of us do this, the result could be a reverse pandemic.

109

Pay the person's toll who's in line behind you.

You might start a chain reaction, or at the very least, make someone smile.

110

Bring a nice hot meal to an elderly neighbor or to a friend who's just had or adopted a baby.

Spend some time with them and offer to help out with any chores that need doing. The most mundane and simple tasks can feel like mountains to an elderly person or to someone who's overtired.

111

Learn when to keep quiet.

Take a break and give yourself the luxury of listening to someone else speak.

112

Send positive thoughts and energy to the people around you.

You'll get it back.

113

Perform company service projects.

Require employees to volunteer at least three times per year, and offer them time away from the office to do so. Once a month, organize four to ten people to either deliver hot meals to shut-ins or to go help out at a local food shelf.

114

Read with your kids.

Try to find stories about kindness, sharing, giving, love, and thankfulness. Let kids pick out stories they love, and share stories you love with them. Improvise different endings to well-known stories, and see how your kids react.

115

Organize a neighborhood event.

Try to get everyone on your block together to get to know one another. It could be a block party, movie night, holiday party, caroling, kids' night, etc. How about a neighborhood Web site?

116

When you see a friend who's feeling down, go out of your way to help lift their spirits.

Sometimes just noticing that someone is down is helpful in itself.

117

Write down all the things you've accomplished within a given period of time.

Make sure to include things you've done for others. It doesn't matter how small a task was. You'll feel great.

118

Plant a tree.

Attach a memory and time frame to its planting, so in fifteen years you'll look at that tree and remember something.

119

Find someone on a plane that could really use your aisle or window seat, and switch with them.

Flying is stressful. Reduce a fellow traveler's stress, and boost your travel karma in the meantime.

120

Assume the person you're listening to has something of value to say.

What if we assumed that everyone who spoke had a nugget of brilliance in what they were about to say? You could even go so far as to look for that nugget of brilliance—more often than not, you'll find it.

121

Remember that hotel walls are not soundproof.

Respect your fellow travelers and allow everyone to get a good night's sleep by keeping the volume down when you're overnighting at a hotel. Don't forget to keep quiet in the hallways too—long, narrow hallways amplify sound.

122

When you're playing music in your car, keep the volume down.

People outside your car don't want to hear your music, and you probably wouldn't want to have to listen to their music either.

123

Patronize a new local business, and if you like it, tell the owner.

The first sixty days of a new business are so important. Simple words of encouragement from a local patron can fill an entrepreneurial owner with enough energy to make it through another risky day.

124

Show respect to coaches and referees at children's sporting events.

These men and women are often volunteers. Give them the benefit of the doubt. They are doing the best they can and are trying to be as fair as they can under the circumstances.

125

Host a cookout.

There's no better way to build community than by getting people together—and nothing brings people together faster than meat and fire.

126

Pick up the garbage around a full can, and tell someone who can help that the can is full.

One word: germs.

127

Give up your seat to someone else on public transit if the vehicle is overfull.

Stand for a while. You can always use the exercise.

128

Donate your pocket change.

Save up your pocket change in a jar at home. Every couple of months, cash it in at the bank, and then donate that money to a good cause.

129

Take a walk around your neighborhood.

Meet your neighbors, ask strangers how they are, help those that might need some assistance, and share lots of smiles—all while working off a few calories.

130

Play a board game
at a staff meeting.

Nothing creates paradigm-shifting synergy like a rousing game of
Chutes and Ladders.

131

Use spell-check.

A typo-filled e-mail reflects badly on you and suggests that the recipient isn't worth the time it takes to look over your work.

132

Gather information before you vote.

Remember that you're voting for more than just a party or the issues. You're making a choice to elect a person to publicly represent your values and your decisions.

133

Follow the six-car-lengths' rule when driving (in other words, don't tailgate).

You probably won't get where you're going any slower, but you'll certainly get there safer.

134

Bake a treat at home for a friend instead of buying it at a store.

It will make them feel more valued. And your kitchen appliances will appreciate the workout.

135

Be patient with elderly drivers.

Pretend they're your favorite grandma who baked cookies for you when you were feeling down.

136

Buy something from the neighbor kid who's selling stuff to raise money for a good cause.

It helps develop a strong community and it gives a kid a sense of accomplishment.

137

Offer to watch a friend's kids for an afternoon or evening.

Or maybe even for a whole weekend, if you know the family well. If you have children of your own, it's a great way to elicit a similar favor. If you don't have children but want them, it's a great way to practice your parenting skills and give your significant other a hint.

138

When you pull out a pack of gum or mints, offer one to the folks around you.

If you give away all of them so none are left, that's even better.

139

Display, learn, and teach compassion.

You owe it to yourself and your children. If not from you, where else will they learn it?

140

Strive to find common ground.

It may seem trivial or inconsequential, but who knows what might come of it. Perhaps you'll make a new best friend, or bring about peace in the Middle East.

141

Whenever possible, use people's names when talking with them.

There's no music sweeter to the ears than one's own name.

142

If you want to pass someone in the left lane, flash your lights and allow them to move, rather than speed around them on the right.

Rarely does someone choose to stay in the left lane if they know someone in back of them is trying to pass.

143

When traveling with another person, turn down the radio in order to allow for conversation.

You may find you have more in common than you thought.

144

Explore your genealogy, and pay homage to the lives your ancestors have lived.

Maybe your great great great grandfather was a famous Viking (and not the purple and gold kind from Minnesota).

145

Buy only as much as you'll actually eat.

As your mother told you, "There are starving children in Africa." She was right, you know, and you should feel guilty about wasting food.

146

If you dial a wrong number, apologize before hanging up.

But if you forget to apologize, there's no need to call them back.

147

Enunciate.

Share the gift of clear communication. Good diction is a gift to the recipient of your message.

148

Don't cut in line, and always acknowledge when others were there first.

Try and remember: no cuts, no butts, no coconuts.

149

If someone appears distressed, politely ask if they are okay or if they need help.

You will be forever remembered if you help someone out. And you will forever remember someone who helps you out.

150

Always pull over for ambulances and other emergency vehicles.

Not only is it the law, but it gives you the chance to think about those who are waiting for that emergency vehicle to arrive. And don't use the open space in the wake of the vehicle to speed ahead. Let those who were ahead of you pull back onto the road first.

151

Keep an open mind, and treat others as you like to be treated.

Try to picture yourself on the receiving end of what you just said or did.

152

If someone has something in their teeth or hanging off their shirt, politely let them know.

Wouldn't you want to know?

153

Offer a handshake first before going in for a hug.

Giving someone the option allows the nonhugger to make a choice, and it reduces the risk of a cultural faux pas.

154

Don't wear headphones in public.

Headphones shut you off from others and send the message that you're not interested in being part of the world around you.

155

Buy a coffee for the person in line behind you at the coffee shop.

Leave before they can thank you. See if they'll seek you out to express their thanks and their surprise.

156

If you've forgotten another person's name, apologize and then ask them for it.

And if someone has forgotten your name, be understanding.

157

Remove your shoes when entering another person's home, especially if they're not wearing any.

Think of it as an excuse to show off your festive holiday socks.

158

Value all life.

You may want to obliterate that spider with a shoe, but if you pick him up with an index card and put him in the yard, he can live out his short life in peace.

159

Take the whole picture into consideration before reacting to a small piece of it.

Science has taught us that the sum of the parts of any given equation is often drastically different than any of the parts on their own.

160

At least once a year, donate your unused, good-condition household items to charity.

Maybe those items will be just what someone else needs. And you'll have a great excuse to go shopping for something new.

161

If someone mispronounces a word, politely correct them instead of poking fun at them.

Some people say mispronouncing words is a symptom of an avid reader who's read lots of different words but just hasn't ever heard them spoken.

162

If you're traveling to a foreign country, learn a few words of the native language.

You show respect for a culture by making an effort to communicate even a little bit.

163

Show appreciation and empathy for a mother or father struggling to control a screaming child.

Let them know you appreciate their effort or that you've been in their shoes before. See if they need help carrying things or opening a door, or offer to get something for them.

164

Recognize that a person's intelligence, potential, and ability to contribute are unconnected to their physical characteristics.

Challenge yourself to find three things that contradict whatever your first stereotypical impression was.

165

Moderate your walking pace to the people you're with.

If you stride ahead, you're just going to have to turn around and wait anyway.

166

Say hello to people you pass in the hall at the office.

Even if they have that "I'm super busy and important" look to them. Perhaps they're just shy. Your friendly greeting might help them feel more comfortable the next time they see you.

167

Bring home fresh flowers, just because.

They might be for a loved one or just for you to enjoy. Pick them from your own garden, visit a flower shop, or buy them online.

168

If you borrow someone's vehicle, return it with a full gas tank.

This is recommended even if you only drove it a few blocks. Gas is really expensive, so you'll be giving that friend a wonderful gift, and they'll be more likely to loan you their vehicle again the next time you need it.

169

Welcome a new neighbor with a smile, some food, and written directions to the closest conveniences.

It can be really scary and unnerving to move to a new place. You can help someone feel like their new house is truly their home.

170

Ask if it's okay before taking someone's photograph.

Some people feel awkward being photographed, and if you don't know the person, they may worry about what you're going to use the picture for. Help your chosen model shine, and give them a chance to say no.

171

Say hello to ten strangers a day.

Some people may look at you funny, but a few will smile and say hello back.

172

Always be gracious when receiving a compliment.

If you deny the sentiment, you're telling the person who offered the compliment that you don't trust their judgment or that they're wrong. Just say "Thanks!"

173

Unlock the passenger door before you unlock your own.

It will surprise your passenger and make them smile, and they can then unlock your door for you.

174

Ask sales associates how they're doing, and wait for an answer before beginning your transaction.

It's easy to hurry through a store and forget that sales associates are real people, not just automatons. Help them feel valued and appreciated.

175

When babysitting, leave the house looking better than when you got there.

You'll definitely get rehired, and you'll feel good knowing you gave those tired parents an extra hour of sleep.

176

At a restaurant, address your server by name.

Be nice. Your server has great control over what you're about to eat and when you'll get to eat it.

177

Keep quiet during movies, presentations, and other events.

Remember the reason why everyone else is there is that they're interested in the event itself—not in you or your reaction to the event.

178

Water, weed, or mow for your neighbors while they're on vacation.

They may think little fairies or leprechauns secretly live in their lawn, and then they'll feel like kids who still believe in magic.

179

If someone helps you move, buy them lunch or help them with a big task of their own.

Moving is tough, emotional work. Saying thank you with a beer just doesn't cut it.

180

When eating out with a group of people, throw in an extra buck or two.

Your server may have cringed when she saw your big group—so make her night. And just put everything on one bill and figure it out yourselves; it's not that big a deal.

181

If someone you know is extremely ill, share laughter with them in addition to tears.

There is something wonderfully dignified about sharing a laugh with someone who is suffering.

182

When someone passes you and there's adequate space for them to pull in front of you, flash your lights to let them know.

Truckers do it because they make a living out of driving well.

183

Greet people with eye contact, a handshake, or a hug.

Start your conversation off on the right foot, and show people that you appreciate and value them.

184

Find a way to give to the developing world.

There are hundreds of worthy causes and effective organizations to choose from. Search the Web. You can donate without ever leaving your already-developed home.

185

Tidy up your yard.

Plant some flowers. Rake the leaves. Mow the grass. Improve the spirit and look of your neighborhood by starting with your own yard, and then offer to help others do the same.

186

Call for help when you see a stranded motorist.

You don't have to stop and help or put yourself in danger, but do call to notify someone who can help. Don't assume someone else already has.

187

Learn geography.

Impress the next person you meet who is from another country by knowing the name of their capital city.

188

Call your mom and thank her for giving birth to you.

Why is it that the people to whom we owe the most are the ones we acknowledge the least frequently?

189

If someone speaks with an accent, don't immediately ask where they're from.

Ask questions about their interests and their life. You'll eventually find out where they're from if you really must know.

190

Visit seniors in a nursing home who don't have regular visitors.

Offer to share a special talent, such as playing music or demonstrating an art project. A little of your time can make a big difference in the lives of folks who may not be able to get out much.

191

Shop global with a conscience.

Support vendors who promote fair trade and who help developing countries lift themselves from poverty.

192

Bring treats for your officemates.

It doesn't have to be a special occasion. Just bring in some treats to share with everyone.

193

If someone near you drops something, let them know or pick it up for them.

It could be something they really need or that's important to them. You also could save them the horrible panic that happens when you get home and can't find something.

194

Pay attention to the flight attendants when they provide safety information.

Listen even if you've heard the spiel a thousand times. The flight attendants are providing a valuable service, so take two minutes, make eye contact, and at least pretend to pay attention.

195

Drop a note in someone's brief-case or bag that encourages them to excel or that lets them know how much you love them.

What a simple way to give someone a boost. It's unexpected and sets a positive tone for the rest of the day.

196

Hold the door open and let a bunch of people go in front of you.

Especially if you're afraid of what is waiting for you outside.

197

Try to look at yourself from another person's perspective.

Are you a person you'd want to be around?

198

Cover your mouth or excuse yourself whenever you have to yawn during a conversation.

Even if a yawn really results from a lack of oxygen, people still assume it means you're bored.

199

When you're done with a store cart, put it in the cart rack or take it back to the store.

Consider how many cars are dinged, dented, or scratched because someone did not take a few minutes to store a cart appropriately. Your car may be next.

200

At restaurants, encourage others to order before you.

But if everyone is vying to go last, just order the first thing that catches your eye, so your server can move on to the next table.

201

If you receive a gift that you don't need, express your heartiest thank you.

And then do something useful with the gift, such as sharing it with someone who might need it or donating it to a charity.

202

Keep the roadside free of junk.

Never throw or dump any trash out the window or door of a vehicle. Teach your children, grandchildren, nieces, and nephews not to do it either. Keep a bag or container in your car for travel waste, and empty it into a proper trash can when it's full.

203

Before running out for coffee or to pick up lunch, ask your coworkers if you can pick something up for them.

If you're going out anyway, why not save someone else a trip?

204

When an emcee asks you to hold your applause till the end, please do.

Focus and precision are crucial to a successful performance, and no one wants the event to drag on too long.

205

In a crowded area, use the seats for your body, not your belongings.

If you see someone looking for a seat and you have personal belongings on an otherwise empty seat, move your belongings to your lap or the floor, and offer the seat to the person who wants it.

206

Handle the heavy stuff in your grocery cart so the cashier doesn't have to.

You only have to pick up the 50 pounds of kitty litter once a week; she has to pick it up ten times a day.

207

Remember birthdays.

Birthdays are special. Make the people around you feel loved. Call them, write them, and shower them with presents.

208

Offer to donate needed items to a local school or nursing home.

That Scrabble game may be your ticket to heaven.

209

If you see trash on the ground, pick it up and dispose of it properly.

Set an example for others as you perform your good deed for the day.

210

Tip at a bar even when there's no tip jar.

A bartender's income for the night is based primarily on tips. And if you tip well, the bartender may even liven up your drink next time around.

211

Even when you're not in a particularly good mood, be civil to the world around you.

You don't want to be known as the grumpety grump of the grump patrol.

212

Teach your children the proper way to behave in public.

A great life lesson is to learn that there are different behaviors for different circumstances and different audiences.

213

Draw a bath for your spouse or significant other after they've had a long day.

Or offer to make dinner or give them a massage. When someone's had a tough day, something small, thoughtful, and simple can make a huge difference.

214

Stick to general, uncontroversial topics early in a conversation.

No one needs to hear your opinions on politics, religion, or other controversial topics the first time you talk with them.

215

Keep the volume of all things low at night if you're outside or have your windows open.

If you're having a party and you know things might get noisy, give your neighbors some advance notice—or better yet, invite them to the party.

216

If you succeed at something
or win a competition,
celebrate but don't gloat.

Everyone appreciates a gracious winner.

217

Call your grandma and thank her for giving birth to your mom or dad.

We can never repay the debt we owe to our ancestors, but they should hear from us that we're grateful for all they've done.

218

If you're in a crab boat and there's only one chicken neck left for bait, give it to one of your shipmates.

If a storm blows up and the boat gets swept out to sea, your shipmates may be the key to your survival. It could happen.

219

Park in a spot that's far from the entrance to where you're going.

You'll get more exercise and it will save the closer spots for people who need them.

220

When coming in from a day at the beach, wash the sand from your feet before entering the house.

Likewise, stomp the snow from your boots. And if you've been playing volleyball in the mud, you may just want to hose off in the yard.

221

Put things back where you found them.

Taking an extra second to put something back can save others many minutes of searching or cleaning up after you.

222

If you notice headlights on in an empty vehicle in a parking lot, notify a nearby business.

If the person who owns the vehicle needs to get somewhere important fast, you may have just saved them an immense amount of hassle.

223

Ask the shy, awkward, or uncoordinated person on the sidelines to join your game.

They'll appreciate the gesture, and who knows, they could turn out to be your team's secret weapon.

224

Send pictures of yourself and your children to your faraway relatives.

Oftentimes we forget how much people celebrate the smallest changes and advancements in our lives.

225

Spend some time at a library.

Even if you're not really into books, you'll be impressed with the amount of information that is available and the number of people who are interested in learning.

226

Keep your hotel room tidy, just as you would your own room at home.

Be appreciative of the fact that you get to leave and someone else gets to vacuum, dust, and do the laundry.

227

Learn your friend and family members' preferences.

And when they visit, make sure you have items and food on hand that they prefer.

228

Share the last item on a plate, or offer it to someone else.

No matter how much your partner denies it, you know they really, really want that last onion ring.

229

If a friend or neighbor is laid up due to a medical condition, organize friends or neighbors to help out.

Circulate a sign-up sheet to bring meals, run errands, and take care of the ailing person's household chores and yard work.

230

Take off your sunglasses when you're indoors.

You're a lot less likely to walk into a wall if you can actually see where you're going.

231

Pour drinks for others before you fill your own glass.

While you're at it, make the next pot of coffee or buy the next bottle of wine.

232

Stop your car at crosswalks and allow people to cross the street.

Pedestrians have the same right as drivers to use public thoroughfares to get where they're going, so give them a "brake."

233

When standing in a circle talking, open the circle to include others standing nearby in the conversation.

If you have your back to someone, a small step to the left or right can make them feel included without drawing attention away from the person who's talking.

234

When someone asks you to switch seats on a plane so they can sit with a family member or friend, do so.

And if you see a separated twosome sitting near you, offer to switch seats with one of them.

235

Put your change in the receptacle for whatever charity a fast food restaurant is trying to raise money for.

Did you really have big plans for that 31 cents? Many small contributions can add up to something significant.

236

When riding bikes in a group, take turns being the lead bike.

Don't just play follow the leader. When you take turns, everyone shares the responsibility of pace-setting and choosing the route, which means the whole group has more fun.

237

Take a friend out to eat, and pick up the check.

Grab the bill stealthily. If your friend doesn't notice you have it, he can't argue with you about who's paying.

238

Lose with grace.

Humor works too. Earn some respect.

239

If you're in the service industry and something goes wrong, explain the problem to the customer before calling for help.

For instance, first tell your customer "I'm sorry, something has gone haywire with my computer. This will just take a few moments," and then call your manager for help.

240

If you're a manager who gets called to help out a salesperson, address the customer too.

Let the customer know you appreciate their patience. After all, your customers are your bread and butter.

241

Wear clean clothes and deodorant, especially when you're going to be in a crowded place.

Remember that smelling someone else's body odor is a choice, not an obligation.

242

Ask people for their opinion, and listen while they express it.

Even if hearing their opinion doesn't make you change your mind, at a minimum it will give you a deeper understanding of the topic.

243

Say your name each time you talk if you're on a conference call with more than two people you don't know well.

It sounds like a bit of overkill, but if you're on the receiving end of a conference call with not very good equipment, sometimes everyone's voice sounds exactly the same.

244

Leave at the appropriate time so that you don't have to rush and endanger others to get where you're going.

If you arrive a bit early, you can always pop in that new CD you've been dying to hear, or make a couple of cell phone calls that you chose not to make while you were driving.

245

If your neighbors are hosting an event or have their house for sale, go the extra mile to make your own home look nice.

It's a quick and easy way of saying "I'm glad we're neighbors." And they'll likely do the same for you one day.

246

If someone accidentally spills something in a public place, stop and help clean up or go get help.

And if that someone is you, make sure you clean up after yourself.

247

Consider people innocent until proven guilty beyond a doubt.

There's a reason why our court system is based on this premise.

248

If you find yourself binge eating, offer some food to a friend or to a local food shelf.

Put the cream cheese down and back away from the fridge!

249

If you see an animal being mistreated, report it.

The police and the Humane Society are wonderful at helping abused animals.

250

When you answer the phone, state your name.

In one step, you just reduced confusion and introduced yourself.

251

Shovel, sand, or salt your sidewalk and entryway to keep passersby and visitors safe.

Your insurance agent will be forever grateful.

252

Share your umbrella with someone going your way.

Or better yet, give it to someone who looks like they might need it more than you. And if you can, keep an extra umbrella in your car, business lobby, or front foyer.

253

Consider other people before acting on your own agenda.

The positive consequences of completing your agenda might have drastically negative consequences to someone else's agenda.

254

Teach a class at your local community center.

Give the coordinator a call and see what topics they're in need of. Perhaps something you're good at is exactly what they're looking for.

255

Wrap your baby's dirty diaper in something when disposing of it in a public restroom.

Leaving it unwrapped is like leaving the toilet unflushed.

256

Keep your dog on a leash in public places, and teach him not to jump up on people.

Some folks have had horrible childhood experiences with dogs. It can also save you from a lawsuit (or a dry-cleaning bill).

257

Invite your child's friend and his family to join your family for dinner.

You'll feel more comfortable the next time your child asks to play at his house.

258

Leave a tip for hotel cleaning staff.

If you leave all your change, you won't have to worry about setting off the alarm when you go through security at the airport.

259

Understand that shouting at a television in public is inappropriate.

It will in no way affect the activity taking place on the television.

260

Learn from the failures of others.

It instantly turns their failure into a success and reduces your need to judge them as a loser.

261

Try to pronounce names correctly.

Apologize if you mispronounce a name, and make a point of learning how to pronounce it correctly for the future.

262

Begin and end your day with gratefulness and positive thoughts and words.

The first few moments of a given day greatly affect the tone and productiveness of all of the moments that follow.

263

If you eat a meal at someone else's house, clear the table for them when everyone's finished.

Do it without being asked. Even if you only get one place cleared before the host stops you, still make an effort, and be persistent.

264

Donate money to charity.

In the next fifteen minutes.

265

If someone asks for help and you can't oblige, help them solve their problem another way.

Or suggest someone else who might be able to help. Most people are just looking for a solution—where it comes from isn't the issue.

266

Teach your children to speak respectfully to others.

Help them understand the difference between being cute and being annoying. The simplest way to teach this is to model it.

267

Be very careful when you're carrying beverages in a public space.

While spilling coffee on someone's shirt is the beginning of many romance stories, in reality, a spill will likely ruin someone's day.

268

Go directly to the source of your frustration, and take action toward a solution.

The only good "whine" is the kind that comes in a bottle.

269

Open car doors for others.

Especially if you reach the car first or if the other person's hands are full. But beware if you try this for strangers. You might end up under arrest.

270

Propose a toast or a round of applause for the host or organizer at the next party or event you attend.

It's a great way to collectively honor someone. A toast doesn't have to be long or brilliant—simple and sincere goes a long way.

271

Be considerate and respectful to the elderly.

Longevity and endurance deserve respect.

272

When dining out, pick up after yourself.

If you drop a napkin or piece of chicken on the floor, pick it up. If you spill water on your seat, wipe it up.

273

Surprise someone who offers you good service.

Monetary tipping can be done anytime and anywhere. If you're worried about the "tipping rules" for a given situation, remember that no one has ever been scolded or ridiculed for tipping too much.

274

Pay attention to what people around you are trying to accomplish.

And help them accomplish it if you can. There's a good chance they're trying to accomplish the same thing you are. It might be more fun to try to accomplish it together.

275

If your spouse is sick, stay home for an evening of TLC.

Make your spouse some soup and get him or her an extra blanket.
There will be other dart nights at the local Chug and Dance Brew Pub.

276

Tip at least 20 percent.

And if the service is great, tip more than 20 percent. At a restaurant, that money isn't just for the server, it also goes to the cook, the host, and the busperson.

277

If you use the last of something, refill it, or let someone know who can take care of it.

This is particularly important with coffee, even more important with a car's gas tank, and vital for a scuba tank.

278

When someone lets you know dinner's ready, get to the table as fast as you can.

The cook has likely been juggling several variables to ensure they all culminate in the food being warm and wonderfully prepared. You only have one variable: your rear end in the chair at the table.

279

Hold the elevator door for those who are entering or exiting.

Elevator doors don't have common sense or courtesy, but we do.

280

When you attend a fund-raiser, always donate something.

The premise of a fund-raiser is that the fun and the amount raised exceed the work and the amount spent.

281

When someone has a major life accomplishment, take a moment to honor that person.

Think of the mathematical relationship between how long it took the person to accomplish that task and how long it will take you to simply say congratulations.

282

Clear your old food and belongings from the company refrigerator.

Leaving your food in the fridge and never cleaning it out assumes that someone else has to clean up after you. Who is that person?

283

Tell older relatives that you're just like them and proud of it.

Think about the positive characteristics and traits you've inherited from your parents and grandparents, and then thank them for the gifts they've handed down to you.

284

If someone cooks you a meal, let the cook know how much you enjoyed it.

This applies whether the cook is your mother-in-law or the chef at a restaurant.

285

Offer someone a break without being asked first.

Delight in the surprise on their face, and watch for an increased work ethic.

286

If you're house-sitting for someone, clean their house for them.

An hour's worth of vacuuming and dusting can make their return home a delightful experience, especially if they're tired.

287

Think of a book a friend might enjoy, and lend them a copy to read.

If they really like it, let them keep it or pass it along to someone else.

288

If you're late to a performance, be prepared to sit close to the aisle, even if you paid for more expensive middle seats.

Your fellow audience members should not have to get up, change seats, or be otherwise disrupted because of your tardiness.

289

Participate in National Night Out.

Even a brief conversation with the people in your neighborhood can lead to some significant changes in the quality of life where you live.

290

If you see that your neighbor's trash is overflowing, offer to put some of their trash in your bin.

It not only allows them to get rid of some unnecessary trash, it makes the garbage collection person's job a bit easier.

291

When answering correspondence, respond to each specific question asked, and try to respond specifically to that person's needs.

Try to answer with what the person wants to know, not what you want them to hear.

292

Coach a little league team or community sports team.

You don't need to be good at sports, you just need to be available and supportive. Perhaps your role could be working with the kids who are naturally gifted.

293

Think of what a complete luxury it is to have a choice of what to eat.

Hungry people aren't picky.

294

Show respect for your children's teachers, and teach your children to respect them too.

Almost all teachers share these common things: they love kids, they want to help kids learn, and they are underpaid. If you really believe your child's teacher is a bad apple, approach the principal and do something about it.

295

If you see that your server at a restaurant is clearly swamped, be patient.

Someone may have called in sick or the owner of that restaurant may be purposely understaffed as a way to cut expenses. It is almost never because of something that the server did.

296

Know the history of the company you work for.

Learn about the company's founders, accomplishments, visionaries, and triumphs. Try to connect your current situation to the past generations of people who worked hard to provide you with your current job.

297

Learn the names of maintenance workers and cleaning staff.

They often work alone much of the day. Sometimes the folks they pass in the hall are the only people they interact with. Say hello! Smile! Let them know you're glad they're keeping things clean and in working order.

298

Place everything that needs to be laundered in your hotel room on the floor.

Place it all together in one pile to make it easier on the housekeeping staff.

299

Pick up your dog's mess, even if no one saw her make it.

The experience of picking up dog messes gets exponentially worse when it's someone else's dog's mess.

300

Only walk on the pedestrian trail, and only bike/rollerblade on the trail marked for wheels.

Walking and riding are two very different experiences. Combining the two often leads to scraped knees and elbows.

301

Wipe off equipment after you've used it at the gym.

Most gyms supply free towels and cleaner in the workout area. This practice also helps reduce the spread of germs.

302

Chew your gum quietly and with your mouth closed.

If this one seems ridiculously childish, pay attention to how many adults are chewing obnoxiously next time you're on a bus or train. Also notice how wearing headphones can somehow make people forget to keep their mouth shut when chewing.

303

Offer the under-the-seat middle storage to the person sitting next to you.

If there are three areas for two people, assume the other person needs the extra storage more than you, and offer it up.

304

Be patient and speak clearly when speaking with a person who does not have English as their first language.

Picture yourself in a different country with a different language dealing with people who are impatient.

305

Take time to understand the guidelines of donating.

Your trash may not be someone else's treasure. Most reputable organizations have donation guidelines readily available on their Web site or at their drop-off locations.

306

If you go to Benihana, laugh and clap for the poor guy who flips shrimp into his hat for a living.

Think about all the things in life that you do to make your way in the world. If someone else has a job that takes guts and initiative, applaud and support them.

307

Dads: Carry the diaper bag, push the stroller, and look after your kids as often as your wife does.

Not that you need to be keeping track, but if you do, you've got a lot of catching up to do due to that initial "giving birth" thing.

308

Treat the clerk at the quickie mart like he's your favorite uncle.

He well indeed could be someone's favorite uncle, but at a minimum he's doing a pretty thankless job for not much money. Watch how customer service increases as customer civility increases.

309

If you're having a disagreement
over the phone and feel
the urge to hang up,
say so before you do so.

If your goal is to end the call, you can do it without slamming down the
phone in a moment of mindless furor.

310

Applaud for musicians.

Show your appreciation at weddings, galleries, and pubs, in shopping malls, and on the street. They've spent years practicing. Be the person who starts the applause.

311

If you're seated at a table with someone and you notice the sun is in their eyes, offer to move.

Or reposition the chairs or pull a shade. If they continue to squint, offer them your glasses or recommend a good opthamologist.

312

Sometimes it's necessary to eat on the go, but be conscientious about food odors.

If you need to consume your lunch in the office, in a waiting room, on public transportation, etc., skip the sauerkraut, tuna fish, or curry. On the other hand, if someone seems wonderfully interested in what you're eating, offer them some.

313

When you meet someone new in your area, invite them to your favorite local restaurant or a cultural attraction.

Help them get to know the community better and feel more at home. If you want to go the extra mile, make a one-page list of the best places in the area to eat, shop, and have fun.

314

If you see someone looking for a place to sit and you have an empty chair at your table, wave them over and offer them the seat.

If you don't know the person, it's a great way to get to know someone new.

315

Memorize the position of dishes and utensils in a standard place setting.

Next time you're seated at a formal dinner, you won't be the one who grabs your neighbor's bread plate or water glass and confuses everyone seated with you. It also will make you seem "refined," and help anyone around you who isn't familiar with table etiquette.

316

When at a lunch or dinner meeting and seated with your back to the speaker, turn your chair around to face the speaker.

That way you won't be twisting around during the speech, or turning your back on the person seated next to you.

317

RSVP promptly to invitations.

Waiting until the last minute may give the impression that you're holding out to see if a better offer will come along. You'll also be of great assistance to the person who's planning the event.

318

If your neighbor's barking dog or loud music is bothering you, talk directly to them about it.

See if you can resolve it together before complaining to other neighbors or involving the authorities.

319

Learn about cultural and religious holidays other than your own.

Wish a happy Rosh Hashanna, Eid al Fitr, Mexican Independence Day, etc., to your friends from other cultures.

320

Volunteer serving meals to the homeless at a shelter.

Think this suggestion is overused and oversuggested? Well, have you ever tried it? If so, when was the last time?

321

Surround yourself with positive people.

People you respect and want to be like—and who practice civility each day.

322

If someone you know has failing eyesight, introduce yourself when you first address them.

You may think that because someone with impaired vision knows you well, they'll recognize your voice. But this is not always the case, especially in a room filled with lots of people or noise.

323

Take an elderly relative or neighbor out to coffee or lunch or to a concert.

An outing may brighten their day, especially if they're no longer able to drive.

324

Be as knowledgeable and prepared as you can when traveling by air.

There are many Web sites and other information sources available that explain how to travel smart. If you're not a frequent traveler, do what you can to get up to speed on the dos and don'ts of airport etiquette.

325

Don't bite your nails and spit them on the floor.

Permanently removing parts of your body and disposing of them is something that warrants being done in private.

326

Be gracious and grateful when your ex gets remarried.

Gracious because you taught them everything they know, and grateful their new spouse is the one who has to teach them still more.

327

Scrape the snow off all the cars on your block.

It will allow your neighbors to enjoy fifteen extra minutes of their morning, and it will initiate a wonderful mystery about the secret neighborhood windshield wiper!

328

Thank the police officer for calling attention to your speeding.

She's just doing her job, and she may have saved your life. You'll also double your potential for getting a warning instead of a ticket.

329

If you have to curse, choose silly words over offensive ones.

Choose words like "snicker doodles," "snap," "crummy buttons," or "fiddle dee dee." You're not likely to offend anyone in hearing distance, and it may help lighten the moment.

330

Argue a point, not a person.

If you disagree with what someone has said, don't regress to personal jabs. Instead focus on the point of the disagreement. Name calling and stereotyping is reserved for children, politicians, and the media.

331

If you bring a child with you
to a restaurant, bring toys
to keep them entertained.

And by all means, pay attention to them. Remember that the other
customers are there for a good dining experience, not to interact with
your children.

332

Take off your hat indoors, especially when eating.

Even if it's just a fast food joint. It honors your dinner partners and the food. And your hair does not look that bad!

333

If you're traveling with a colleague, have a conversation with them.

Don't just focus on your computer screen or your Blackberry. Take the opportunity to learn something new about your colleague.

334

When you respond to an e-mail, use the person's name.

It's much nicer to receive a message such as "Hi Jen! I received your report," as opposed to "Yeah."

335

At a party or networking function, make an effort to speak with people you don't know.

They might be new to the group, and might turn out to be the most interesting person you've ever met.

336

Make double-sided copies.

Save a few trees and a few bucks the next time you make copies for a meeting or presentation. Many copiers make this task as easy as the press of a button.

337

Give thoughtful gifts.

Find out what a person really wants and then satisfy their wish. The extra thought and effort really counts!

338

Don't shout at your children from across the room.

Walk over and talk to them quietly, face to face. You'll save everyone involved a lot of embarrassment.

339

Be respectful of other people's personal space.

Leave a little room between yourself and the person in front of you when you're standing in line. Crowding in line is rude and makes everyone uncomfortable—not to mention it adds to the spread of germs and crabby attitudes.

340

When trying on clothes in a store's dressing room, hang the items you don't want back on their hangers.

Don't just leave them wadded up in the dressing room. It makes a mess for the next customer to deal with, and it's no picnic for the salespeople to clean up. Also, those balled-up clothes might get permanently damaged, which ultimately contributes to higher prices.

341

Use humor appropriately and with consideration.

All great comedians understand their audience first. If your goal is to get a laugh, understanding what your audience thinks is appropriate is a must.

342

Care for things as if they're irreplaceable.

For many things in this world, and certainly for the people, this is the truth.

343

If you're jogging on a sidewalk, move around other pedestrians, rather than expecting them to move for you.

The horizontal diversion will increase the number of muscles you're exercising and decrease the possibility of repetitive-behavior bone attrition.

344

When someone ahead of you is loading items into bins at the airport security area, wait until they're completely done before you put your bin on the belt.

Remember they need to place their shoes, belts, and laptop in a bin too.

345

If someone looks lost or they're staring at a map, ask if they need directions.

Most likely they're a tourist or visitor, and there's no better way to let them know how friendly and civil your community is than by offering them directions to where they're trying to go.

346

If you're taking an elevator to the top floor of a building, send it back down after you reach your destination.

81.63 percent of all elevator rides begin on the first floor.

347

If you visit a great restaurant or read a thought-provoking book, share your good experience.

Many small business owners and authors don't have the money to afford large marketing or advertising campaigns. Word-of-mouth can go a long way—and the Web makes it easy for anyone to spread the word.

348

When driving during or after a rainstorm, be aware of road puddles near pedestrians, and try to avoid splashing people.

It's hard for anyone to enjoy their day after they've been doused with a gallon of roadkill soup.

349

Ask your older relatives about their childhood, record their stories, and share the recording with your siblings.

Like most things in life, there's a finite amount of time to do so.

350

If you notice that someone appears to be cold, offer them a jacket or turn up the heat.

If they're too warm, offer to turn on a fan or open a window. It's pretty hard for someone to be fully engaged in what they're doing if they're focused on their physical discomforts.

351

Spend an afternoon at a museum.

Whether it's history or science or art, dive deep into something that's completely apart from your job or your typical day.

352

At a restaurant, assume that the host is trying to find you a table as quickly as possible.

Try not to keep asking every five minutes if something is available, or glaring at the host until he calls your name.

353

When you're bike riding and want to pass someone, give advance notice.

For example, say "On your left," and thank people when they move over.

354

Avoid putting your children in trying situations that test their patience.

Be aware of their limits and help them succeed at being well behaved.

355

If you're on the phone with a customer service worker who is helpful, thank them personally.

And then let their manager know how helpful they were. Many times the call is being recorded, so your positive comments may really help the person who was helpful to you.

356

If you get put on hold during a phone conversation, stay by the phone while you're waiting.

Don't wander away and leave the person on the other end thinking that you hung up on them. Besides, you might never learn the answer to what you called about.

357

Take extra money you're going to spend on super-sizing at a fast food restaurant, and give it to charity.

You lose weight and your money helps other people!

358

If you're sitting in the middle of a row of seats, be mindful of how many times you get up.

Proper planning can prevent poor performance! Every time you get up, you make everyone else get up too, to let you by.

359

Commit to learning basic personal information about five people you work with.

For example: name of significant other, name of children, place of birth, place of current residence, college or high school attended, hobbies, etc.

360

Cheer for your own sports team rather than jeering the opposing team.

If you enjoy jeering the other team more than celebrating your own team, perhaps you should get season tickets to the opposition's home games so that you can express your opinion about them on a more regular basis.

361

Know the history of the city you live in.

One of the things governments do well is record the past. There's plenty of accessible information available, and after a couple hours, you can increase your pride about where you live by knowing its past.

362

Offer to collect your neighbor's mail while they're out of town.

It helps the postal worker on your route and protects your neighbors from being targeted by thieves.

363

If you're in a hurry at a restaurant, let your server know in advance that you're rushed.

Ask what menu items can be served the fastest, and ask for and pay for your bill as soon as your food arrives.

364

If you pick up something in a store and then decide not to buy it, put it back where you got it from.

The less time the store's employees have to spend replacing items to their proper spots, the more time they'll have to help customers find what they need.

365

Take a CPR certification course.

Theoretically, if everyone knew CPR, no one would ever die. Wait. Okay, now you can laugh.

Afterword

Thank you so much for reading our little book. Everyone at the Brave New Workshop hopes you enjoyed it. Remember what my wife Jenni told me: "They're not trying to be rude, they're just forgetting to be civil."

Keep this book in a convenient place and take it out when you need it. We hope it energizes you to think of new ways to increase the civility of our world, and if you do, be sure to go to www.speedoflaughterproject.com and help us write the next volume of *Return to Civility*.

Thank you!

John Sweeney and the Brave New Workshop

Contributors

Thank you to the following Brave New Workshop staff who contributed to this project in many ways, big and small:

Lauren Anderson	*Mike Fotis*	*Dave Jennings*	*Katy McEwen*
Brian Aylmer	*John Haynes*	*Lynn Lanners*	*Julia Schmidt*
Joe Bozic	*Dawn Hopkins*	*Jenni Lilledahl*	*Stephanie Scott*
Erin Farmer	*Elena Imaretska*	*Caleb McEwen*	*John Sweeney*